An Older Person's Guide
to
Life and Laughter

Neil Browning

An Older Person's Guide
to Life and Laughter

Neil Browning

ISBN 978-1-917109-32-1

A CIP catalogue record for this book is available from the
British Library.

First Edition – June 2021
Second Edition (Extended) - March 2024

Published 2024
Tricorn Books, Treadgolds
Bishop Street
Portsmouth PO1 3HN
www.tricornbooks.co.uk

An Older Person's Guide
to Life and Laughter

CONTENTS

CHAPTER 1
INTRODUCTION

Whatever you can do, or dream you can, begin it
Boldness has genius, power and magic in it.
(Johann Goethe)

The above is the principle I was guided by when I wrote this book. It's a book about seeing life from an older person's perspective. Things are different when you get to 'our age'. The younger ones probably think we're 'past it' – perhaps we are, in some ways. In other ways, we know far more than they do – about things in general, but more specifically, about life and how to face it. They may be the ones who've 'been there' and 'done that' and they're now wearing the teeshirt, but we've been there, done that, got the teeshirt, took it back because it didn't fit and got our money back. Why? Because we knew we could, and because we'd complained before and 'got a result' as they say these days.

This then is a miscellany of thoughts about life from an older person's perspective, with a particular emphasis on humour. You could say it's a cornucopia of items. In fact I had to look up cornucopia because I wasn't sure if it was quite the word I was looking for, and it's significant that I went straight to an online encyclopedia rather than a dictionary. That's important you see, it means I'm trying to keep up with all the computer technology rather than being what the young ones would probably call old-fashioned. However, in this case it back-fired because online I found out it was a horn of plenty originating from Greek mythology, and that wasn't what I wanted to know – you see, we don't always get it right. The dictionary was much better, that said: 'A large supply of different things'.

Somebody said that age is only a number you can't change; well, I believe that too, so stop worrying about it and learn to live with it. We senior citizens have a big bonus – a wealth of experience, and it's the most valuable experience of all – experience of life. Life itself is stressful, (we've found that out at first hand), but that doesn't mean that now you have to wallow in stress, you can learn to rise above it and deal with it, and you should be able to come out on top, maybe not every time but often enough to make it worthwhile – hopefully this book will help you to do that.

This book essentially represents a personal view, but I have tried to make it interesting, thought-provoking and above-all humorous, because, let's face it, humour is a valuable aid to getting us through life. It takes far less muscles to smile than to frown, so now you know which one to do – but I suspect you knew that already. As for laughter, that has been shown to reduce the levels of stress hormones in the body. Two doctors in the U.S. have a theory that 'beta-endorphin-like compounds released by the hypothalamus activate receptors on the endothelial surface to release nitric oxide, thereby resulting in dilation of vessels' (To some people, there's nothing like using ten words when one will do!) However, it is true that there are sneaky little things called endorphins, and they're important because they're feel-good hormones which are released into the brain when you're doing things you really enjoy. So now you know what to do: start doing things you really enjoy and get your fair share of endorphins!.

Now we're at the age where we can sit back and take it easy;

we've earned the right to do that – don't have a conscience about it. Alternatively maybe you can pursue a hobby or special project that you didn't have time to do before. (That's what this book is for me - see quotation above). Sit back and let the others do the rushing around – it's more satisfying when you know you don't have to do it. (Joke: I hate doing nothing – you never know when you've finished.)

So, I hope this book will make you laugh and make you think. Believe me, the youngsters haven't got it all their own way. At our age, life can be much more satisfying.

A tribute to Spike Milligan

I suppose I should start this book 'With apologies to Spike Milligan'. But why? They say imitation is the sincerest form of flattery, and that is exactly how this book is meant. 'I'm sorry Spike for imitating and/or flattering you". How does that sound? Fairly ridiculous I'd say. He'd probably think so too – and say it in no uncertain terms; he was renowned for speaking his mind.

I hope he would have liked my thoughts, jokes and poems – I hope you do too. This book is supposed to be a tribute to the man, penned as such in my humble way. I'm not trying to emulate him - no-one could possibly do that! Inevitably I suppose I have put my own stamp on it. Will it be first-class or second-class? (Sorry, I just couldn't resist that!). No doubt you will make up your own mind, Dear Reader (as Spike would have put it) by reading this book and buying it or not buying it.

One way of reading it without buying it is to smuggle it out of the shop surreptitiously concealed up your jumper. If you are contemplating this I should inform you that this doesn't usually work. (We wont go into how I know that or how much experience I base this judgement on). Even if you're in a cheap shop that can't afford those sneaky little three-foot high contraptions on either side of the doorway, the chances are that an even sneakier security guard who hasn't caught anybody for weeks will chase after you down the street attempting to thoroughly embarrass you thus: 'Oi my good man, I 'ave reason to believe you 'ave a copy of that excellent and very readable book 'An Older Person's Guide to Life and Laughter' concealed about your person! You: 'No, I haven't, honestly!' Him (or her): 'Look 'ere mate, I wasn't born yesterday!' You: 'No, you look about 72.' Him (or her): 'It's a lie I'm only 59. Anyway, I 'ad surreptitiously concealed myself be'ind the Autobiographies when I espied you secretin' the aforementioned harticle under your coat'. You: 'It's all lies, it wasn't under my coat it was up my jumper.' Him: 'Ah ha! Cough it up then'! You: 'How can I cough up a book when it's too big to fit in my mouth?' Etc etc and so on and so fifth.

In my opinion Spike was a genius. That's not easy for anyone as I personally believe it's a very fine line between genius and madness.

So here we go. You've seen the book, you've read the film, you bought the teeshirt and took it back because it didn't fit. Now, drop everything (no, not that Min, that's the best china! And pull those knickers back up at once!) Get comfortable, have a gorilla (no thanks, I've just put one out), stop straining with that trowel and wallpapering those knees! Oh and if you're reading this late in the evening, cover up the budgie and send Granny to bed. (Note: if it's easier, cover up Granny and send the budgie to bed).

CHAPTER 2 –
POEMS IN THE STYLE OF SPIKE MILLIGAN

The Cloud

I wandered lonely, I'm a cloud
That floats o'er hills both high and low
'Til all at once I saw a crowd
Of people on the ground below.

I thought now I will play a game,
And so on them I made it rain.
Great big drops and sploogee sploshes
But none of them had mackintoshes.

I rained on hairy and bald heads,
They were annoyed with me, they said
'Little cloud, we won't forget
You rained on us and made us wet.'

So I moved over in the sky
To let the sunshine make them dry.
They said 'That's not enough, you see
You made us late home for our tea'.

'We're not amused, its not a joke,
Tops, trousers, knickers, we are soaked.
You made puddles that we trod in,
Shoes and socks, all now are sodden.'

I'm just a fluffy little cloud
Who should be free to roam
But you see
They captured me
And put me in a home.

The Banana

Why does a banana have such a lovely taste?
It's a pity that the skin of it always goes to waste.
And how about the its shape, now is there anything forlorner?
It always looks as if it's trying to go around a corner.

The Peach

I tried to pick a luscious peach
But it was just beyond my reach
The reason here is plain to see
As I am only five feet three.

Chipping Sodbury

In this life of doubt and pain
Shall I see Chipping Sodbury again?
Prob'ly not, but let me say
I've never been there anyway.

Alternative verse:
In this life of doubt and pain
Shall I see Chipping Sodbury again?
Prob'ly not, but let me say
I didn't like him anyway.

British Knees

Rise up British people! We should celebrate
The wonders of the British Knee before it is too late!

Stout knees, British Knees, these knees won the war!
Knees atop stout British shins that go down to the floor.

Strong knees, wiry knees, knees with sinews many.
That's why the Germans lost the war, their knees hadn't any!

Firm knees, active knees, leaping all around
Helping you do somersaults six feet off the ground!

Charging up and down steep hills or running for the bus
These knees support our hairy legs, not needing any truss.

Though your knees are wrinkly and they make others howl
Don't cover them but show them off, just like Baden-Powell.

A barrier to all disease for this they are renowned:
Stop Athletes Foot from going up or dandruff coming down.

They also can protect your legs by curing rising damp
Which otherwise creeps up your legs and gives you night-
time cramp.

Knobbly knees triumphant have won many a contest.
It's well-known throughout the world:
BRITISH KNEES ARE BEST !!!!

CHAPTER 3
PHILOSOPHICAL PROSE

This Chequered Life

Born we are
Thrust into this chequered life,
So ill-equipped
To face its trials, tribulations and pressures

'You must do well at school'
Taxes, bills, money worries
A serious illness in the family
The death of a loved one
Or 'Its not working out between us, I think its best we part'.
Like bad dreams that wont go away.

But we surmount them
By going through them
And getting over them, still smiling
It's hard, but we are learning something:
How to face up to adversity
Maybe next time the hurt will be less

Who are we?
What are we?
What will they label us?
(Why do they label us?)
They labelled Spike 'manic depressive'
What does that mean?

For him it meant big black holes that he hated but couldn't
    get out of.

But in the end the bad things are outweighed by the good:
A child's laugh
A kitten at play
A rainbow
A sunset
A glorious country view
Holding hands
A smile, an 'I love you' meant just for you
All these are ours for the taking
And we need to take them
Because they make the bad times better.

Hidden Talents

We all have hidden talents.
We owe it to ourselves to find these and use them
Before it's too late
If we don't
How will we know
What we could have achieved?

We all have personal things that we should say to loved ones
We owe it to ourselves
To say these things to them
Before it's too late
If we don't
How will we know
What they might have replied?

CHAPTER 4
QUICK-FIRE JOKES

We've all been in a pub with friends and everyone's had a couple of drinks. The chances are that when there's a lull in the conversation, someone will tell a quick-fire joke. These are some of that kind of pub-type quick-fire joke.

I walked into this Chinese restaurant and I said 'Do you do take-away?' He said 'Yeah, six take away four leave two'.

I booked into this grotty little hotel and the bloke in reception said to me ' Tell me sir, do you have a good memory for faces?' I said 'Yes I think so, why do you ask?' He said 'Well, the room I've put you in hasn't got a shaving mirror in it.'

I went into W H Smith and I said to the girl behind the counter 'I'm writing a letter to my girl-friend and I want some nice posh notepaper to write it on'
She said 'Do you want it scented?' I said, 'No, I'll take it with me'.

I've just bought this dog. I call it my DIY dog 'cos its always doing little jobs all over the house. It's very clever, it even makes things; last week I gave it a boot up the backside and it made a bolt for the door.

There was one time when I didn't speak to my wife for 6 months – well, I didn't like to interrupt her.

Patient: "Doctor, I've got chronic amnesia."

Doctor: "How long have you had it?"

Patient: "Had what?"

I phoned up the Council, I said 'Can I have a skip on my drive-way?'

They said 'It's your drive-way, you can skip where you like.'

I miss my ex-wife quite often – but my aim is getting better all the time.

By the way… you may think some of these jokes are quite old – and you may well be right. But I can tell you these jokes have been told to the Queen. And when they were told to the Queen she laughed so hard, her tiara fell off. Mind you, Prince Albert didn't think they were funny at all.

CHAPTER 5
INTERESTING TRIVIA

Business origins

Everybody's heard of B & Q but what do those initials stand for? They stand for Richard Block and David Quayle, the two people who founded the firm in 1969, in a disused cinema in Portswood Road, Southampton.

Tesco, currently the largest supermarket in the UK, was named when its founder, Jack Cohen, bought a consignment of tea from a firm called T E Stockwell. He 'fused' his name and theirs together. Asda is formed from the first 2 letters of the words Associated Dairies. It was formed in 1969 and is currently the second largest supermarket in the UK; the third is Sainsbury's.

Google

The word google is derived from the word googol. A googol is the number 10 to the power of 100 which can be written as a 1 with 100 zeros after it. Google is the biggest and most popular search engine in the world; it accesses 40 billion pages of information and it handles 9 billion searches every day. A billion is a thousand million (1,000,000,000). A billion used to be a million million, it has now been 'downgraded' to a thousand million. Note: I googled Google to get this information!

'The Archers'

The Archers is the world's longest-running drama series, having run for 19,200 episodes. It started on the 1st of January 1951.

Guinness Book of Records

This is a source of loads of trivial records, the following ones are some of the quirkiest:

Fastest time to swap the engine in a VW Beetle (team effort) : 1 minute 6 seconds.

Fastest time for a dog running 5 metres backwards: 6.73 seconds

Largest pizza : 13.5 square feet.

Largest number of people at one time in one place keeping a hoola-hoop going for two minutes : 2,496. A further 514 people also competed but either dropped their hoops or allowed them to go too low down their hips; they were thus disqualified.

And last but not least : Most baked beans eaten in 3 minutes with a cocktail stick (team of 4 people) = 429.

Words

I love words, so forgive me if I run on a bit about them.

The word bus is a shortened version of omnibus which is a Latin word meaning 'for all'. Thus it was a mode of transport which all could use. The first buses appeared in France in 1829 and in London in 1833.

What do you think is the origin of the drawing room? After all, you don't go in there to draw do you? This is another shortened word, it was originally the withdrawing room, where the female members of a dinner-party would withdraw to have a chat leaving the men at table smoking cigars and drinking brandy, after which they would rejoin the ladies.

The word data is plural; a single item of data is a datum (the origin of these is Latin). The word graffiti is also plural (its origin is Italian). A single item of graffiti is a graffito.

The plural of the word base is bases; the plural of the word basis is also bases but it is pronounced (phonetically) as 'basees'. Similarly, the plural of axe is axes; the plural of axis is also axes but pronounced 'axees'.

The plural of stadium is stadia and for forum its fora (both from Latin). However these plurals (and others) have both been anglicised to stadiums and forums, and both plurals now appear in dictionaries.

It occurs to me that if there is a record for the number of different ways of pronouncing the same set of letters appearing in different words, that might be held by the letters 'ough': think of though, bought, plough, rough and through.

A butterfly was originally called a flutterby.

Ha-ha, ell and jejune are all words in the dictionary. A ha-ha is a barrier with a ditch in front of it, constructed in such a way as not to impede the view beyond it. An ell is a unit of measurement. Jejune is an adjective meaning empty or devoid of substance.

Long, long ago the phrase 'God be with you' got shortened to 'God be wi' ye'. At a later date (but still ages ago) that phrase became shortened again to one word: Goodbye.

There are no words in the dictionary which rhyme with orange, purple or silver.

Duck quacks
Duck quacks don't echo. No-one knows why.

Bruce Lee
Bruce Lee moved so fast that when filming him they had to slow

the camera down. This is the opposite of what usually happens, i.e. they have to speed things up.

Longest words

The longest word in English dictionaries used to be 'antidisestablishmentarianism', (defined as opposition to the disestablishment of the Church), but a while ago it was beaten into second place by 'floccinaucinihilipilification' (the estimation of something as being virtually worthless), and that has now been overtaken by 'pneumonoultramicroscopicsilicovolcanoconiosis' (a supposed lung disease). There are longer words but they don't count as they are medical descriptions, and not vocabulary words.

Collective nouns

These are many and varied but all interesting and some quite hilarious.

A group of owls is called a parliament. A group of crows is a murder. A group of penguins is a huddle or a waddle. A group of swans on land is a lamentation, but if they're in flight it's a wedge. A group of ducks on land is a waddling; if they're in the water it's a paddling, and if they're in flight it's a skein. You couldn't make it up could you?

A dog's nose

A dog's nose is much more sensitive than a human's. But expert opinions vary widely as to how much more sensitive it is. Some experts reckon it's only 10 times more sensitive but others reckon it could be a million times more sensitive. Not much discrepancy there then! Whatever it is, it accounts for their ability to sniff out drugs and such. Dogs rely heavily on smell; no matter how clean we humans keep ourselves, we're always 'smelly' to a dog and dogs rely on that to recognise their owner and to distinguish one human from another, because to them each one of us has a distinctive aroma!

Centralia

You may have seen this on cable TV (that's where I got it from!). In Pennsylvania in the U.S. there's a town called Centralia. In 1962 the inhabitants had to move out; it had to be totally evacuated because it was unsafe to live there. It was built over a coal mining area; they had been burning some rubbish in the town and somehow (nobody knows quite how) the flames got into the ground and started igniting all the coal seams, thus the town became too hot and too dangerous to live in. There is no way of stopping the fire; it will keep going until it either runs out of air or runs out of coal, and nobody knows when that will be, it could keep going for up to 250 years! Until then, Centralia is a ghost town.

Owls

An owl can't move its eyes, but it can turn its head up to 270 degrees. Actually, that affects the circulation to its head but it has a system that keeps its blood circulating when necessary. Some owls have such good vision that they can catch and eat prey in the darkness.

Internet Origins

The Internet, arguably one of the greatest-ever inventions, was created in 1989 by a scientist called Sir Timothy Berners-Lee, and he was (wait for it…) **BRITISH!** (Cries of:'Jolly good, I say what a clever fellow' etc etc…) He was knighted by the Queen for this and his other work in computer science. The Internet is now being accessed by 53% of the total world population; that figure is higher for the developed countries – 86%.

Real names of celebrities

We've all heard of Reginald Dwight (Elton John) and possibly Diana Fluck (Diana Dors). Cary Grant was Archibald Alec Leach. Tom Cruise is Thomas Cruise Mapother IV. Freddy Mercury came from Zanzibar, his real name being Farrokh Bulsara. Ben Kingsley is Krishna Pandit Bhanji. The pop singer Dido's real name is (wait for it): Florian Cloud de Bounavialle O'Malley Armstrong. I think I can see why she shortened it now!

The American actor Walter Matthau was really Walter John Matthow. However, he was a lover of practical jokes, and started a rumour that his second name was Foghorn and his last name was Mattuschanskyasky. Before long everybody believed it, to such an extent that he even got credited under his 'long' name in one of his films. Note, that's about the same level as my sense of humour too – he was a man after my own heart!

Have you ever wondered how 'Sting' the leader of the pop band The Police got his strange nickname? I did. His real name is Gordon Sumner. Early on in his career he played with a group called the Phoenix Jazzmen and frequently wore a sweater with black and yellow hoops on it. Somebody said he looked like a wasp, and thus the nickname was born.

Daft song lyrics

Back in the 60's I distinctly remember a song with the daftest backing-lyrics I'd ever heard; these were: Gobble diddle it, gobble gobble diddle-it, hey! It was Turkey Trot by Little Eva; actually it was quite a good song apart from those awful lyrics.

There's a song by Cher which has similar lyrics, though not quite so bad. Due to these it has acquired a different title: it is now referred to as: It's in his Kiss (The Shoop Shoop Song). By the way, Cher's real name is Cherilyn Sarkisian. Just thought you'd like to know.

Pi

Pi is defined as 'the ratio of a circles circumference to its diameter'. It is usually written as having the value 3.14159 but this is only correct to five decimal places. Its true value when written as a decimal never ends. Not only that but the successive numbers in its value don't form any kind of recurring pattern. Due to this strange and wonderful (!) situation it has been used to test the abilities of super-computers in accurately calculating it. Its value has been calculated to over 70,000 digits (!) and even that does not express it accurately, as at that point it hadn't ended . (Don't you wish you had that amount of spare time?)

Longest song title

In 1970 the pop group Fairport Convention put out a single called 'Now be Thankful' whose B-side had a title 38 words long. This was an attempt to get into the Guinness Book of Records for the longest song title ever, which it did for a while. However, this was spotted by another pop group who promptly put out a single which had a B-side with a title 53 words long.

Kelloggs Corn Flakes

The idea for corn flakes began by accident. John Kellogg and his brother Will left some cooked wheat to sit for a while to attend some urgent matters at the sanatorium where they worked. When they returned the wheat had gone stale, but in an effort to save it they forced it through rollers thinking they would get long sheets of dough.

To their surprise, what they got were flakes, which they toasted and served to the patients in the sanatorium. This was way back in 1894. Kelloggs cereals are now made at Trafford Park, Manchester, which is the largest cereal factory in the world.

Strange but true.

If you take a mathematical quantity of any whole number (even as low as 1) and take away half of it, then progressively take away half the result (0.5, 0.25 and so on), in spite of the fact that you are reducing the total each time, you will never reach zero.

Origins of words

To eavesdrop on someone is to be close enough to them to hear their conversation, even if they can't see you. Literally the word refers to the side of a house, and being close enough to the house so that if it was raining you could stand under the eaves and thus not suffer from water dropping off the eaves, i.e. you would be within the eaves-drop of the house. I assume (though I don't know) that this refers to thatched roofs and was in use before the advent of guttering.

The phrase 'there will be the devil to pay' refers to boat-building In the construction of wooden hulls of small boats, each plank of wood was separated from the next by a length of oiled or waxed rope, which had to be 'paid in' between the two planks and fixed tightly so that the joint remained waterproof.

The last plank was always the most difficult and so it was referred to as 'the devil', thus paying in the last length of rope was the most difficult part of the job.

CHAPTER 6
LIMERICKS

There was a young typist named Mabel
Who seemed to be mad and unstable
She would swing from the lights
Dressed in pink spotted tights
And then she would dance on the table.

There was a young lady from Gweek
Who with men was not winsome nor meek
She would say 'If you're rude
Or try anything crude
I'll kick you right into next week'.

There was a young diner at Crewe
Who found a dead mouse in his stew.
Said the waiter ' Don't shout
Or wave it about
Or the rest will be wanting one too!'

There was a young lady named Jenny
Whose underwear items were many
Bra's, slips, panty-hose
She had plenty of those
But knickers, she never wore any!

There was a young lady called Janet
Who came from the Isle of Thanet
She said 'One day, I swear
I'm going back there
I've just got to sit down and plan it'.

There was a young man from Caerphilly
Who wandered about willy-nilly.
One day on a stroll
He fell down a big hole
And he said to himself 'That was silly'.

An archaeological lady from Penge
Who'd gone down to visit Stonehenge
Said 'I'm shrugging my shoulders,
They're such great big boulders,
How on earth did they stand them on end?'

An athletic young fellow from Preston
Had trouble when putting his vest on.
One day (don't you laugh)
It split right in half
And he said "Now that's taught me a leston."

An elderly fellow named Spike
Said to someone he'd met on a hike
"You may not like me, though
Do not mock the Goon Show
Or I'll say something you may not like!"

A lovely young girl called Victoria
Was found in a state of euphoria.
Her man, back from lunch
Had said "I've bought a bunch
Of all these lovely flowers for ya."

An artistic young man from Tibet
Painted pictures outdoors and got wet.
He said "Oh, what a caper!
It drenched my art-paper
And I haven't dried it out yet."

A stay-at-home lady named Pat
Needed exercise 'cos she was fat.
She said "It's raining torrents
The weather's abhorrent,
There's no way I'll go out in that."

A couple of young girl East-Enders
Went out on the worst of all benders.
They drank whisky and gin
And then got run in
Because all they had on were suspenders.

NOTE:This verse may need some explanation:

Dictionary-type definition of ' Bender':
'Bender' (noun):
A tour of the majority of local hostelries involving the
consumption of liberal amounts of a wide range of alcoholic

beverages, resulting in a state of serious inebriation, and in the worst cases also some affectation to vertical equilibrium.

This may also include a degree of unlawful merriment including the possible removal of certain items of clothing.

My definition:

A booze binge.

Dictionary definition of 'Run in':

'Run in' (verb):

To be subjected to a somewhat forceful invitation which is being effected by a law enforcement officer on an unsuspecting member of the public to attend an interview at the offices of the local constabulary involving questions and largely incoherent answers, the main purpose of which is to establish beyond reasonable doubt whether or not a 'bender' has taken place, and, if so, whether or not the individual(s) concerned were implicitly involved. In the more serious cases this may also involve an overnight stay at the afore-mentioned establishment, allegedly at 'Her Majesty's Pleasure' (though to date there has been no concrete evidence to show that Her Majesty is aware of individual cases).

My definition:

Having your collar felt.

A footloose young fellow named Jim
Went to Venice one day on a whim.
He wrote back to his pals
'It's all flipping canals,
To get anywhere you have to swim'.

If you want to write limericks, I'm
Sure that you'll do it in time.
Work hard, 'fore you know it
You'll be a great poet,
You've just got to make the things rhyme.

CHAPTER 7
LOVE POEMS

Safe to Shore

I'm helpless on the sea of life
Emotionally sore
I need to see safe harbour
And to stand firm on the shore

I am alone and drifting
Can see the land no more
No ships on the horizon
To help me reach the shore

But now at last I've found you
The one that I adore
And you will be my life-line
And steer me safe to shore

For now you're here to guide me
I'm foundering no more
You are my compass and my chart
You'll see me safe to shore

The ocean's swell may toss me
Fear'd as in days of yore
But you're my raft, my hope, my life
With you I'll reach the shore

The birds they fly above me
On updraughts they do soar
I'll be uplifted by them
As you steer me safe to shore

The flotsam and the jetsam
Will trouble me no more
For you will steer me through it
And see me safe to shore

The pounding waves upon the rocks
A vision I abhor
No more will be my enemy
For I'll be safe on shore

You've caught me fast and lifted me
My trials they are but o'er
Bruised and battered, tossed and turned
You've brought me to the shore
On losing someone dear

It's true we don't appreciate
What we have had 'til it's too late
That applies to people too
But with some effort I'll get through
All the sorrow and the pain
With any luck I'll smile again

Losing you was hard for me
But as time passes I can see
Things in a very different light
Though I miss you both day and night
It's true I grieve with furrowed brow
But life is not so different now

Even though I'm on my own
I know that I am not alone
Perhaps all this was meant to be
In contemplation I can see
You are still here in spirit, all
Our happy memories I recall

The prophets say, when someone's lost
You should not sit and count the cost
But rather think of what you've done
Of treasured memories now won
Not of hopes and plans and fears
But of highlights through the years

I think of what we've done together
Not of bad or stormy weather
But of bright sunshiny days
Together-times I'll keep always
The many places we have been
What we've done and what we've seen

Nature's wonders are still there
For me to marvel at and share
A stunning sunset, evening hours
A garden full of gorgeous flowers
A waterfall, a butterfly
A quiet lake, a mountain high

Your radiant smile I see again
In my mind it will remain
Your laughter too I treasure now
The many friends we made, and how
You picked me up when I was down
You have not gone, you're still around

The main thing which I really feared
Has not happened, you're still here.

Us

We are now one together, we were lonely while apart
We share our thoughts, our hopes, our dreams, for you now
    have my heart

We'll share the quiet moments, we will not need to talk
For there will be the chemistry between us as we walk

We'll have such plans and schemes, we'll talk about them
    from the start
Achieving them together which we could not if apart

It is written in the heavens that we should be together
Sharing everything we are and being one forever.

CHAPTER 8
QUIRKY QUOTES

Mondays are a really bad way to spend one-seventh of your life.

All those who believe in the power of the mind, raise my hand.

I almost had a psychic girlfriend but she left me before we met.

I know the speed of light, but what's the speed of dark?

When everything is coming your way, you're in the wrong lane.

Hard work pays off in the future. Laziness pays off now.

Everyone has a photographic memory. Some just don't have film.

If a drug addict takes an 'upper' followed by a 'downer', does he end up back where he started?

A shin is a device for finding furniture in the dark.

I intend to live forever - so far, so good.

What happens if you get scared half to death twice?

I used to have an open mind but my brains kept falling out.

If at first you don't succeed, destroy all evidence that you tried.

Experience is something you don't get until just after you need it.

For every action, there is an equal and opposite criticism.

No one is listening until you make a mistake.

Success always occurs in private, and failure in full view.

The problem with the gene pool is that there is no lifeguard.

The sooner you fall behind, the more time you'll have to catch up.

A clear conscience is usually the sign of a bad memory.

If you must choose between two evils, pick the one you've never tried before.

A fool and his money are soon partying.

Plan to be spontaneous tomorrow.

If you think nobody cares about you, try missing a couple of HP payments.

If it's not illegal, immoral or fattening – go ahead and DO IT!!

Drugs may lead to nowhere, but at least it's the scenic route.
I'd kill for a Nobel Peace Prize.

Bills travel through the mail at twice the speed of cheques.

Borrow money from pessimists - they don't expect it back.

Refunds of money always take four times as long as you expect.

They say you should grow old gracefully − well I plan to grow old DISgracefully − it's much more fun that way.

You only have one life - LIVE IT!

CHAPTER 9
SONG LYRICS WORTH REPEATING

I'll stand by you... even in your darkest hour...
Wont let nobody hurt you...
Nothing you confess could make me love you less
(The Pretenders / I'll Stand by You)

(I) came a thousand miles just to catch you while you're smiling
(Jethro Tull (Ian Anderson) / Reasons for Waiting)

If you feel you've had too much of this life. hang on...
You're not alone... Take comfort in your friends
Everybody hurts sometimes – everybody cries...
Hold on, hold on...
(REM / Everybody Hurts)

The sun is up, the sky is blue, it's beautiful and so are you
(Lennon-McCartney / Dear Prudence)

Times of joy and times of sorrow, we will always see it through
I don't care what comes tomorrow, we will face it together
The way old friends do
(Abba / The way old friends do)

The more we learn, the less we know
(Lennon-McCartney / The Inner Light)

Beauty I've always missed with these eyes before….
Just what the truth is, I cant say any more
But I love you… Oh how I love you….
(The Moody Blues / Nights in White Satin)

And in the end, the love you take is equal to the love you make
(Lennon/McCartney / The End)

CHAPTER 10
REMEMBER WHEN.... (Reminiscences)

Petrol Cost

Remember way back when petrol cost so much less than it does now? I had a job on the forecourt of a petrol station which was situated on the Exeter By-pass. This was way back before self-service had come in. It was also way before the M5 got there – at that time the Exeter by-pass was notorious for its long traffic-jams.

Petrol then was 6 shillings and 7 pence a gallon; 3 gallons cost 19 shillings and 9 pence - just under a pound. People would come in, get 3 gallons and say to me 'Keep the change' ! Today, by my calculations, (4.5 litres to the gallon and about £1.19 a litre) that would be 13.5 litres, costing roughly £16 at today's prices. That's inflation for you!

At that time I had a Hillman Imp and had parked it in a corner of the forecourt. A lady I had just served said to me 'Is that your Hillman Imp over there?' I said it was. 'Oh' she said, 'can you tell me where the choke is?' She hadn't had her car long and so far she had failed to find it. Not totally surprising as, being a rear-engined car it was sneakily situated on the floor next to the gear-stick, a fact which I explained to her. 'Oh, thank you' she said, and drove away, presumably happy in the knowledge that from then on she would be able to start her car more easily on cold frosty mornings.

There were drawbacks to that job though. A few cars had narrow petrol pipes and there was no such thing as a sensor or automatic cut-out on the pumps. If you got one of those cars, whammed the nozzle in and started pumping at full power, the petrol would blow back and drench your shoes and the bottom of your trousers, resulting in trousers and feet smelling of petrol for the rest of the day and a mess on the forecourt which you had to clear up! Worse, the customer could then complain that you'd wasted some of the petrol and refuse to pay the full price! In practice that almost never happened, most people just had a good laugh about me getting drenched!

DIY Shops

Do you remember when there were small DIY shops that sold exactly what you wanted? It was before the days when everything was pre-packed – you could go in and ask for, say, 15 one-inch size 8 screws. Not like now, these days you either have to buy 50 or a pack of 500. And their floors were just plain floor-boards, no carpets at all. I'm not sure why, but that's invariably how it was.

I remember having a brilliant 'friendly-banter' type relationship with the man who ran our local DIY store. I went in one day, he was there with his back to the counter. I said 'Good morning' He replied in the same vein. Then he turned round, and said 'Oh, if I'd known it was you, I wouldn't have been so polite' Lovely stuff, you never get that kind of thing in B & Q, do you?.

Change – pipes & cylinders

Way back (I can only just remember this myself) shops didn't have automatic point-of-sale computers. The check-out person had to work out the cost of your items, check it to ensure you'd paid enough and then they took your money, folded any notes and stuffed it all into a small cylinder which they put into a tube, then pulled a handle, which propelled it rapidly up the tube to somewhere at the other end of the store. It reached a person there who took the money, checked it, recorded it and then worked out your change (if any was due) and sent it back down the tube to your sales-person.

Meanwhile you were standing at the checkout twiddling your thumbs (or whatever) and listening for the noise in the tubes which signified that your change was coming back. Of course, if the store was busy and your luck was out, it was usually someone else's change coming back and you had to wait longer for yours!

Cheese-cutting

In the days before cheese was pre-packed, you could go into the butcher's and ask for the type of cheese you wanted and the exact amount you wanted (for example 'about half-a pound'). Then the shop assistant would bring out a cheese-board with a wire cutter and cut off the amount you asked for. The amazing thing was, they would always get it right to within a few pence (that's old pence of course).

CHAPTER 11
A GUIDE TO ECONOMISING

This is inevitably a subject dear to all our hearts. Unless you really set up your pension correctly when you first started it up (remember that far back? – no, neither can I!) you probably haven't got as much coming in now as you expected. If you're anything like me, it's probably less than you need. Anyway we all need to economise: remember the old saying 'Look after the pence and the pounds will take care of themselves'? Updated to take account of inflation, I would say that these days it's more a case of 'Look after the single pounds and the fives and tens will take care of themselves'.

Shop around to save money on the expensive bills, in particular gas and electric. Using a net comparison site I once got a quote of about £25 a month less than I was paying before. Admittedly it was an 'online-only' service, so it's wise to be PC-literate or to learn how if you're not already. There are many local day or evening classes to enable you to learn the necessary skills. If you're not good with computers (or mobile phones for that matter), ask other members of the family – in particular, don't forget that these days teenagers in particular are all experts at that sort of stuff, and are a fountain of wisdom as far as us 'oldies' are concerned! Comparison websites can be useful for insurance too (car, house etc) but beware the added cost of instalments.

In particular, if you live on your own and you haven't already done it, phone your Water Company and ask for a water meter to be installed. It is one of the easiest things to get done these days; I had it done recently and it was quick, easy and totally painless. Not only that, but within 2 weeks of getting it, I got a nice refund on my water bill; what more could you ask for from a public utility supplier!

Also, it's a personal view, but I like to think it's not a good idea to be a slave to your central heating clock. By that I mean that if you're feeling a little cold and the heating isn't due to come on for a while, put a jumper on – old-fashioned but effective and it may solve the problem. After half-an-hour, if you're still cold, then put the heating on – you've still saved money. And don't forget to buy an electric blanket (assuming you haven't already done so) – getting into a warm bed makes such a difference, especially during the winter.

Don't pay exorbitant car parking charges if you don't have to. If you can, park a couple of streets away and walk. This gives you a bonus of getting some exercise at the same time. Mind you, it doesn't work too well if it's raining or you have loads of shopping to get!

Always ensure you get a good deal from your suppliers. If your TV service doesn't work properly, (which can be serious at our time of life!) and you can't watch it, even if it's only 24 hours, phone up the supplier and complain. Play the Senior Citizen card – in this case it's justified – if you get it right, you may well get £5 off the bill for a day's outage. If you are fed up with generally bad service, listen for the ' If you're thinking of leaving us' option on the phone; that's exactly the place you want to be. These are the people who are authorised to knock money off your bill. It works both ways: they don't want to lose you and you don't want the hassle of moving to somebody else. Make a note of the Customer Service phone numbers for all your suppliers and keep them somewhere safe. This will avoid you having to dig up old documents to find them, thus saving time and hassle in an emergency.

CHAPTER 12
INVENTIONS WE DIDN'T KNOW WE NEEDED

The following are things which have been invented during our lifetime. We didn't know we needed them at first because at that time they hadn't been invented – but afterwards we realised we couldn't do without them – and now looking back we wonder how we managed to live without them before!

Remote controls for the TV (and other things)
We used to have to get up out of our comfy chair and go over to the TV to change channels, or even just to turn the volume up or down! What a pain that was – and what an improvement this is!

The M25 (and other motorways)
It's true we did need the M25 (however did we get round or through London before it was there?) But we didn't know then that it would turn into the 'longest car-park in the world' did we?

The Internet
Well this is questionable. You may think that the Net is the greatest thing since the invention of sliced bread or baby-doll nighties (depending on what sex you are). It certainly has great advantages – just finding out about information generally - if you're anything like me you probably never bought an Encyclopedia Britannica, even if you were encouraged to buy a set by a door-to-door salesman - or buying stuff you need and having it delivered without you having to traipse down to the

shops, possibly in the pouring rain.

On the other hand, it has sneaky ways of getting you to buy stuff you definitely don't need, often without you realising that you've done it until the cost appears in your bank account. Note: the sneaky wording is usually buried in their Terms & Conditions – do you ever read those? No, neither do I – they're always at least 30 pages (i.e about 60 screens) long!

Electric Blankets

What a great feeling it is on a cold winters night, to climb into a lovely warm bed and toast your (probably cold) toes at the same time! And all for only the cost of 15 minutes of electricity (which isn't enough to notice on your bill anyway). Fantastic!

Before electric blankets, you had to climb into a cold bed and warm up your cold extremities on your bed-partner – and you would almost certainly get a good telling-off for doing that.

Mobile Phones

Soon after these were invented, I remember passing people in the street who appeared to be talking to themselves. I thought this was very strange, until I realised that they were in fact talking into their mobile phones!

How did we ever manage to get things done while we were on the move before these crafty little gadgets arrived? Not to mention finding people when you weren't sure where they were. Oh, and getting an amazingly accurate local weather forecast for up to 10 days. I used to wonder how my mobile always knew where I lived – until I found out that it works by pinpointing where you are and juggling signals from about three local network masts.

Microwave Ovens

These are a terrific help to males like me who only know the rudiments of cooking and have trouble cracking an egg without breaking the yolk. I know its got to be hot but I have not the least idea how long it will take. Microwave oven plus instructions on food packet equals success! Also a full stomach – not necessarily of the right food but food nevertheless, and it's a great improvement on what we used to cook – i.e. beans on toast.

Washing Machines

These are a fantastic help and time-saver for helpless males (again, like me) who live on their own. They not only wash your clothes but they think for you as well, which saves you both time and brain-power. My machine has about 15 different programs and all you have to do is turn a knob to get the right one (I use 'Daily Wash' even if I only need to do it once a week). Also it only needs two other buttons to be pushed to get it going. So you only have to worry about putting the right amount of fluids into the right compartments to start off with, and I manage to get that right most of the time. Oh and my machine plays a pleasant music-box tune when its finished.

Satnavs

A boon for lonely males on long drives, though less so if they haven't managed to get Joanna Lumley's voice on their particular Satnav. However, when they first began to be available there was a headline story about the driver of a large delivery lorry who followed his satnav instructions to the letter and ended up in a narrow lane sandwiched between two hedges and unable to move. I think the manufacturers improved them a bit after that.

Personal Computers

Amazing little machines. All the more amazing when you think back to the days before microchips and all that sort of thing had been invented. In your laptop now, you have the same sort of power which back in the 1960s would have taken up a whole room-full of IBM computing-power. IBM was known as 'Big Blue' then, due to the size and colour of its computing equipment. I happened to be working for them then; ironically, they didn't rush to get into the Personal Computer market when these were first launched. I think it was too much of a change for them and they wanted to see how things panned out and let others be the 'guinea-pigs' if the machines didn't achieve what they were supposed to.

CHAPTER 13
COMEDY POEMS

Pills

Have you ever stopped and thought
About those tablets you've just bought?

How wonderful are all our pills
They treat a myriad of ills
Cure more things than you could guess
And all this on the NHS!
All of different shapes and sizes
Some come from Penge, some from Devizes.

But some have side-effects so nasty
Some come on slow, some come on fasty
Some painful, make you scream and shout
Others make your hair fall out.

It's true that they are not all good
Some don't work just as they should
One man gave them to his daughter
Lost much more weight than she oughter

She got thinner than a rake
'Stop' said Dad 'for Heaven's sake
Or else in a week or two
There'll be nothing left of you.'

All these wondrous tablets they go
On treating warts, spots and lumbago,
Almost every known disease
They even kill most kinds of fleas

Regulating temperature
Not too cold or hot
Except for making coffee
They do the flippin' lot!

A Yokel's Lament

One day when it were rainin' buckets
I thought meself 'With any luck it
Will stop soon.' Norm'ly I don't give two hoots,
I gets me mac and welly boots
And goes out gardenin', like a duck
I'm 'appy as a pig in muck.

I grows a lot of veg and flowers
But this day t'were them scattered showers
I'm not a dunce, I'm pretty fly
So started on some DIY.
The smell of gloss do make I feint
So I used that emotion paint.

As I weren't in a 'mediate rush
I used me big long-'andled brush
And started painting all me walls
(Don't use a ladder, 'case I falls).

You has to mix it careful, see,
To get the right constituency.

When done, open yer windows wide
So the air do get inside
Otherwise tis best to mention
You'll get lots of condescension.
I done it all in grassy green
Bestest job you ever seen.

I called my wife in when I'd done,
She stood there lookin' rather glum
I thought with her t'would be a hit,
But did 'er like it? Not one bit!
So one day soon when it do rain
I'll 'ave to do it all again!

My Menagerie

I have a mouse
And he lives in my house
Behind the skirting board.
I think he's got a hoard
Of food in there
With enough to spare.
I know he's there
But I don't know exactly where
He is,
So I can't catch him.

I've got a goat
He's got a bad throat
He coughs a lot
I've told him not
To do it.
He knows that he should use a handkerchief
But he doesn't.

I've just bought a cow
And now
I can't work out how
To get it through my doorway.

I've got a horse
It doesn't live with me of course
That would cause me stress
And I would get a mess
On my best
Carpet.

I've got a frog
And he lives in a log
But he's gone the whole hog
And invited all his family in.
I don't mean to be unkind
I wouldn't mind
But they croak all night and it keeps me awake.

I've got a cat
He's never sat

On a mat
How un-proverbial
Is that?

I've got an elk
Or something of that ilk
It doesn't give me any milk
But anyway
I'll let it stay
Cos I can easily get all the milk I need
From Tesco's.

I've got a Lesser-Spotted Wild Bolivian Ant-eater
He doesn't stay in the house, I keep him in a shed at the
bottom of the garden.

I used to have a whale
It's such a sorry tale
I think I really oughter
Have put a lot more water
In my pond for him
To swim
In.
But I didn't.

I've got a mother-in-law
Last time I saw
Her she had acne.
I don't visit her much now. My fear

Is that she'll want to come round here
And visit me
I hope she doesn't.

I've got a pygmy shrew
I wish I knew
What trials I'd go through
There was a lot of trouble brew-ing.
He ate up my whole washing line
And all the clothes on it, which at the time
I needed.
How he got up there I will never
Know. Perhaps he thought that he was being really clever.
But I didn't.
I've got a Duck-Billed Platypus
I'll let you think of a rhyme for thatypus
'Cos I can't.

I've got a toad
It just gives me a load
Of trouble.
It used to play
Every day
With the goldfish in my pond.
I thought it was very fond
Of them,
But now it eats them.

I've got a girl-friend
I'm at my wits' end

She complains about the rules
Concerning all my animules
And how I feed them.
Though she'll prob'ly scream and shout
I may well kick her out
And get another one in
Then perhaps there'd be more fun in
My life.
Or would there?

I bought a snake
But I won't make
The same mistake
Again.
Truth is he's no fun
Just lies there in the sun
Won't play with a ball
Can't climb up a wall
And he can't sing
Or dance or anything
Like that at all.

I've got a Sabre-Tooth Tiger
Comes from somewhere up the Niger
River.
I can definitely say
He keeps all wrong-doers at bay
He also keeps out others who
I like - the postman and the vicar too.
I hope that he decides to stay

And not escape and run away
Into town and run amok
Molest someone and cause havoc
'Cos then where would I be?
In jail.

I've got two lovely daughters
I don't see them like I oughter
They have busy lives you see
So they don't come to visit me
As often as they could
I wish they would.

So this is me
And my menagerie.
You can visit if you like
Though if you come by bike
It's quite a hike
But still
I will
Be very pleased to see you.

Postscript

You may think
This kind of verse
Is very terse
And you might
Be right.

I write most of it at home
When I am on my own.

I wrote some in the hall
That wasn't good at all
Draughts in that situation
Disturbed my concentration.

I wrote some in the conservatory
That was purgatory
'Cos at the time
It wouldn't rhyme.

I wrote some in the yard
That was hard
'Cos it came on to rain
What a pain,
I won't do that again.

But it has to be said
I never write in bed
Because I can't write properly when I'm lying down like that.

CHAPTER 14
A GUIDE TO LIVING ON YOUR OWN

It is one thing to decide to live on your own; it suits many people. But it is quite another to be thrown into that situation, as I was, by the death of a loved-one. If that is your current situation, believe me, I would not presume to tell you how to live, but the following are some rules or ideas that I have found useful when the grieving, quietness and boredom gets to me, as it has done recently, what with Covid and bad (i.e. depressing) weather. If just one of these appeals to you and/or helps you then I shall have done a Good Thing in passing it on to you and I shall feel happier having done someone else some good as a result of my own experience.

Dig out all your old CDs and DVDs and put them by the hi-fi and DVD player (you may have to leave aside the ones which have too many memories). Whenever the house seems too quiet, put a CD on, In the evening if there's nothing on TV that you like, put a DVD on instead. Personally I don't like daytime TV very much, so I record loads of programmes on evening TV and play that back whenever I feel like it. Bonus: Some of the programmes I record are 2 hours long, but when you play them back you can whizz through the adverts, and that way they only take about an hour and a half.

They interviewed a 105-year-old woman on TV recently and asked her the secret of her long life. She said 'I always try and find the positive in everything'. Do that yourself. For example, from 21st December the days started getting longer; Covid is turning the corner and vaccines are being distributed NOW.

We WILL get back to (more or less) normal living sometime SOON. Spring is not that far away, so that will bring better weather, cheer us up with lots of new flowers and enable us to get out more.

As well as being positive, always look for humour wherever it is to be found. For example, I order my dog's food on the Net: it is Harringtons Wet Dog Food (Variety Pack). However, most description fields in Net programs can't handle that many characters; hence, if I check my order after I have put it in, the system tells me I have ordered a Harringtons Wet Dog! While I was walking the dog a few days ago, a van drove past me; the business sign on it said 'Sherwood Florist'. Brilliant humour!

Never miss a chance to get out if the weather is looking even half-decent. I believe there's no substitute for fresh air and exercise; I make a point of taking the dog out for about an hour every day if possible. The exercise is as essential to me as it is for her (I have Parkinsons). I am a bit of a 'sun-catcher'; I like to spend time just sitting in my garden when the sun is out, and I eat breakfast or lunch out there whenever possible. Bonus: As you probably know, sunshine gives you lots of vitamin D which is good for you.

Always cultivate endorphins. Look them up on Google if you don't know what they are (as I did when I first heard of them). In a nutshell, they are feel-good hormones that get released into your brain automatically when you are doing things which you really enjoy. We need as many of those as we can get in our situation, and it's especially important to know how to get them! In amongst all the routine (i.e. boring) chores etc, try and spend some time every day doing something you really enjoy. Pursue your favourite hobby or pastime or even start a new project. For example, I have recently printed A4-size copies of all my best digital photos and put them in two folders to look at and show to visitors, I have also written this book, which I immensely enjoyed doing, so of course I got a lot of endorphins through that! In addition to all this, last Christmas I sent out jokey Christmas cards to people I have met on dog-walks 'From my dog to yours'.

Use the Net when it saves you time and/or effort in having things delivered to your door, but don't let it get to you when things go wrong as they often do online. I also use online banking to do direct transfers of money to family members or to pay irregular bills online and the money moves within a couple of hours without the need to go to the bank.

I am currently having fun fending off scam phone-calls (yes, FUN). I have had a lot recently and they used to annoy me, but now I recognise them immediately for what they are and enjoy sending the callers away with a flea in their ear. Basically, if you treat them like very pushy double-glazing salesmen, you can't go far wrong! For example, I told one recently that he didn't work for BT Openreach any more than I did, also that he was part of a scam and I had found him out. I also tell them I have reported them to the Police (which is true, I have reported them to Action Fraud) and threaten them with dire consequences if they dare to ring me back - so far none of them have! Bonus: It gives me a sense of achievement and of justice, as they are getting exactly what they deserve. Also, they are treating me like an idiot, telling me they have English names when they are obviously foreign, and ringing me from Virgin media, when I am a Sky customer! I dial 1471 after every call and note the numbers which I then pass on to Action Fraud in case they can trace them.

Each Christmas, dig out all your light-up decorations from the loft and put batteries in them. If you're anything like me you may have forgotten how good they are and how much they brighten up your home when they're switched on.

Always keep enough food in so that you have a choice of meals and are not restricted to just one. That way, if you have had a busy (or bad) day and don't feel like cooking you can always find a quick meal to pop in the microwave. Also, don't forget takeaways – our local Indian restaurant does the best Indian food for miles around and their take-aways are just as good. Personally I like to alternate my bread between 50/50, wholemeal and rolls so as to get some variety; I get two different cereals and two or three kinds of biscuits for the same reason. Make sure though that you eat properly and look after yourself diet-wise. I am a bit of a choc-a-holic so I do tend to buy too much chocolate, cakes and sweet stuff generally, but I do exercise enough will-power so as not to eat them all at once – my cholesterol level is high enough already! Also, I know that ultimately my body wouldn't forgive me for that, and neither would my GP if he knew I'd been stuffing myself with chocolate and gooey cakes!!). I absolutely love beetroot and lettuce, so I improve my diet generally by putting those with everything I possibly can! Also, I 'make bargains' with my conscience; for example I will allow myself a second cake or sweet item for dessert if I eat some fresh fruit first, and I will allow myself to sit longer outdoors in the sunshine provided I am up-to-date with my household chores indoors.

Don't let the weather rule your life but do take account of it in planning your days.

Personally I like to check the weather forecast in advance on my mobile phone and if necessary adjust my dog-walking and shopping for when its fine. Conversely, if the weather is bad, I use that time to catch up with indoor chores or activities. That way I don't miss out on any fine weather that happens to come around, also (bonus!) the dog and I are much less likely to get caught out in an unexpected downpour.

Indulge yourself, you are struggling through a difficult time and you should pat yourself on the back for getting this far (assuming there's no-one else with you - if there is, get them to do it!) Make sure you buy yourself the food and drinks and chocolates you like best for Christmas in case nobody else gets them for you. Don't beat yourself up if you make a mistake or get into a bad situation because of something you forgot. We all make mistakes and you are almost certainly going through a bad time, so the chances are that your brain is not functioning as well as it should.

Have a realistic attitude to life and luck, and don't forget the old saying 'You can't win them all'. Realise that sometimes even your best-laid plans will go astray and don't let it depress you if they do. I enjoy bidding for items on Ebay auctions (it gives me a 'buzz'), but if I don't get them I try and think (for example) that I wouldn't have bid that high as I don't think the item is worth that much anyway. Also, the same thing may come up again in the future at a more reasonable price, so all is not lost.

If you are making journeys, allow extra time for hold-ups, roadworks etc. If being late for an appointment or getting behind time causes you stress, do what you can to avoid it beforehand. Personally, I don't regard shopping as a chore, it is an opportunity to get out of the house and it's quite possible I may meet one of my neighbours and so be able to socialise at the same time. Any heavy shopping I let the supermarket deliver to me so that I don't have to carry it home.

Of course, one big advantage of living on your own is that you win all the arguments which may occur in the household! Actually, that's not strictly true; in my case I do lose the odd one or two arguments with my dog, and the odd two or three with my conscience!

Don't worry if you start talking to yourself or indeed to inanimate objects (e.g. ' Come on kettle, hurry up and boil, I haven't got all day!' or 'For Heaven's sake, computer, surely it doesn't take you this long just to access Google?'). On a more serious note, of course it's absolutely normal to talk to lost loved ones.

Lastly be a bit philosophical. There's a well-known saying: 'Whatever you can do, or dream you can, begin it. Boldness has truth and magic in it.' (Goethe). Always look for something new which you will enjoy trying. That gives you a new interest and a new positive incentive which should help to cheer you up. I have an idea to brighten up my driveway which I want to do as soon as the weather improves in the Spring. No-one has done this before and I think it will look just great when I have finished it – it is easy and wont take long. In an odd hour go onto the Net and Google 'Quotable Quotes'. There is a whole mass of wit and wisdom there on subjects like Life, Love, Humour, Self etc. You are bound to find something that you can relate to, adopt and/or cheer yourself up with.

Personally I have Parkinsons so can't drive now but it is under control (which means I don't mind taking the 7 tablets a day which it needs) and it doesn't limit me a lot at present; I don't let myself get depressed with it (not easily anyway). Apart from that I have fairly good health (for a man of 70-something or-other!). I can still get about with my bus-pass and taxis, so I am not as bad as many other people I know. I can still live a perfectly good life; I have good family and friends to support me but I have the satisfaction of knowing that I can handle life on my own. There are many others far worse off than me.

Above all, stay strong, stay positive and stay healthy.

CHAPTER 15
SOLITUDE

I was on holiday in Cornwall once many years ago, and I remember walking along the Coastal Path somewhere near Coverack, though the location is not important now. I was walking along the cliff edge and I saw a bay with a beautiful beach, possibly half a mile long. There was a long flight of steps leading down to it and I decided to go down and enjoy the situation. Some people were coming up and we exchanged hellos as we passed.

It occurred to me then that they had been the only people on the beach and that it was now totally empty. I got to the bottom and drank in the wonderful sensation – the sun was out and it was lovely and warm, perfect beach weather with a perfect situation and a perfect view. It was one of those times when it seemed that all the elements which I loved , the weather, the sea and the scenery, had come together just to please me. It was perfect solitude - I felt it was my beach, and my beach alone and I owned it, at least for a while.

A small boat came into view and I thought 'No, you cant come in here, not now, I want to be on my own, it's my perfect beach and you'll spoil it for me...!' It must have heard me, because it went away.

I lay on the beach and revelled in the whole situation. It was peace, perfect peace. I didn't have to be anywhere else or do anything else (not that I would have wanted to anyway). It was just me alone and communicating with Nature. I thought how lucky I was to be able to be there and to enjoy it so much. Many people can't walk so could not get there, many have lost their sight so could not see it, and many their hearing so could not hear the waves lapping on the beach. I was lucky enough to be able to do all that and I felt so grateful and lucky to be given that situation and that perfect day.

It was one of those extra-special occasions that everyone should be given at least once (but preferably several times) in their lives. I hope that some day I will get another time like that. It was indeed an especially memorable time for me − it was so special that I have never forgotten it.

CHAPTER 16
MORE JOKES

What men and women say – and what they really mean

Men

I'm going to the allotment = I'm going to the pub.

Another pair of shoes dear? = For Heaven's sake, you've got more than Imelda Marcos already.

Is that a designer handbag? = It looks like something Dolce made while Gabbana wasn't looking.

I'll do that in a minute dear = I'll do it when I've finished watching the football / the motor-racing / Marilyn Monroe on TV.

I don't think that outfit really suits you my love = I can't afford it.

I'll fix that soon = I'll fix it when I'm good and ready, and not before. Anyway it's been like that for ages.

I don't think that colour suits you dear = Your bum looks big in that.

Is this the grocery bill? = HOW MUCH? You must think I'm made of money.

Women

Are you going to put those trousers in the wash? = If you don't change them soon they'll be able to walk to the machine on their own.

How about you doing the washing for a change? = There is

no 'laundry-fairy' my love, it's really me that does it all the time.

Do you love me? = I'm going to ask for something really expensive.

We need to talk = I need to complain.

Do what you want = You'll pay for it later.

How much do you love me? = I've just done something you're really not going to like.

Questions and Answers

Q: How do you know when it's Christmas?
A: It's when the dustmen start talking to you

Q: What do you call a deaf parrot?
A: Anything you like, he can't hear you.

Q: What's the definition of mixed emotions?
A: It's when you see your mother-in-law backing over a cliff in your new car.

Q: What is a beetroot?
A: A potato with high blood-pressure.

Q: What is it called when a man is married to only one woman?
A: Monotony.

Q: What is a cannibal?
A: A man fed up with people.
Q: Complete the following proverb: One good turn....

A: Gets all the blankets.

Q: What lies on the ground a hundred feet up in the air?
A: A dead centipede.

Q: Why do birds fly south for the winter?
A: It's too far to walk.
Q: Name five animals from the polar regions.
A: A seal, a walrus and three penguins.

Q: What is the difference between an Indian elephant and an African elephant?
A: About three thousand miles.

Q: Who was Karl Marx?
A: He was the fifth one of the Marx Brothers

Q: In which battle was Admiral Nelson killed?
A: His last one.

Q: What is a piece-de-resistance?
A: A French virgin.

Q: What is avant-garde?
A: A French chastity-belt.

Q: What animal got off the train at the wrong London terminus?
A: Waterloo Bear.
Q: How do you tell the difference between a weasel and a stoat?

A: They are weaselly distinguishable because they are stoatally different.

Q: Where do you take a horse when it's ill?
A: To horsepital.
Q: What's round and very bad-tempered?
A: A vicious circle.

Q: What is Italy's best-known export?
A: Sophia Loren.

Q: What lies on the sea-bed and shivers?
A: A nervous wreck.

Q: What is an acquaintance?
A: Someone you know well enough to talk about but not well enough to speak to.

Q: What do you call a cat who has just swallowed a pillow?
A: A duck-filled fatty-puss.

Q: What do you call a drunken ghost?
A: A methylated spirit.

Q: What is pizza?
A: It's the place with the Leaning Tower.
Q: What do you get from a pampered cow?
A: Spoiled milk.
Q: Where do you find a dog with no legs?
A: Right where you left him.

CHAPTER 17
DON'T YOU JUST HATE...

Parking spaces that aren't big enough for your car?

You've got to park your car centrally in the space, otherwise you might not be able to get out of one side or the other. That means you might have to have two tries at driving into the space properly. Even then you've got to be careful getting out, otherwise you may hit the door of the car next to you. Is it any wonder there are so many cars about with parking blemishes on the paintwork? And to cap it all, you're probably paying a fortune for the parking space anyway!

Packaging you can't undo?

DVDs and CDs come wrapped in cellophane – I haven't yet found an easy way yet to open these. There's nothing to get hold of, and you can't use scissors either. On a packet of biscuits they give you something to tug, so at least you stand a sporting chance of getting it open first time. I don't know why they can't do the same with these.

But the worst ones I've found are those that are packed in thick heavy-duty plastic packaging, like small DIY tools or kitchen utensils or stuff like that. You know the kind I mean. They don't give you any indication at all of how to open them. You can't use ordinary scissors because the plastic is too thick, so you've got to use heavy-duty scissors. It's never obvious where to start so you just have to try the best you can. And even if you do manage to get in you can still draw blood trying to get the thing out of the packet. Let's face it, as far as accessing the items inside goes, this kind of packaging is about as useful as a chocolate fire-guard. If you haven't got any heavy-duty scissors, forget it. Years ago before this kind of packaging was invented I can't remember ever having that kind of trouble opening anything. Is that progress? I don't think so.

Unethical selling?

I find this on the Internet all the time. They con you into getting something 'free' but when you actually go for it, it turns out to be nowhere near as good an offer as you thought because it has drawbacks. How many times have you seen (for example) an offer of '£30 off our range of wines' – it turns out you have to spend more than £60 to get it. But you can't complain because they word it in such a way as to make you believe you will get it but if you look at the wording carefully it turns out they haven't actually promised you anything.   I was buying something on the Net the other day. It inferred that I could get £20 off the item I was buying. It turned out to be an offer for their credit card, which couldn't be redeemed until I'd received the card and activated it. So I couldn't use it to get a discount on the item I was buying, I could only do it on my next or subsequent orders. But it's still possible to get a result - I'm playing them at their own game, I'm getting the card so as to get the £20 discount but I won't use the card at all – I'm not daft, it charges about 30% interest!

Bin liners?

I haven't come across a bin liner yet that I could open at the first attempt – its almost as if they've been glued together before they left the factory. They must have a gigantic air-sucking-out machine at the end of the production line, and once the bin liner has been past that you stand no chance whatsoever of opening it. You lick your fingers to try and prise it apart, and then you remember you've just been cleaning the loo and haven't washed your hands yet. Again, I don't remember having this trouble years ago – if this is progress, take me back to the good old days!

And lastly:

Those automated phone answering messages with so many options that you think you'll never get to speak to a real person.

I get properly fed up with these. So I have decided to record an answer-message on my home phone, as follows:

If you want to speak to me, press 1. If you want to speak to my wife, press 2. I If you want to speak to my children, press 3. If you want to speak to my dog, press 4. If you are a scam phone caller please note that I haven't got any money. If you want to sell me double-glazing, don't press anything, just hang up and go away.

CHAPTER 18
MISCELLANEOUS MUSINGS

Thin joke - fat joke

I am very slim, in fact I'm painfully thin, (absolutely true):

Every time I go to a football match, I have to keep moving about, otherwise they mistake me for one of the goal-posts. A bamboo-cane's got more fat on it than I have.

I wouldn't mind, but every time I take a shower, I have to run around to get wet.

There was this very fat lady – she was incredibly fat – as big as the side of a house, small battleship, Guinness Book of Records job. One Sunday she went down to the seaside and sat on the beach. Trouble was, she took up so much room on the beach, the tide had to wait until she'd gone before it could come in.

The tribal chief

There was this tribal chief, lived in a mud hut, and because he was the chief elder of the tribe he had a big mud-hut with two floors. He was very proud of his status in the tribal village and he had a throne made so that he could receive any of the villagers in style. He was rather elderly and infirm, so he had a hoist put in to move the throne up or down as he needed it so he could receive people upstairs or down depending where he was, having found it very difficult to manage the stairs. One day when the throne had been hoisted up he happened to walk underneath it, and it fell on him and injured him.

The moral of this story is: People who live in grass-houses shouldn't stow thrones.

Butter-knives

You should never start rumours about butter-knives… you know how those things spread.

Animal names

I remember years ago, I went down to our local paper-shop to get a magazine or something. The counter had a see-through glass top, and immediately underneath it was a shelf with the day's papers displayed on it. On the papers there was a tabby-cat, fast asleep. I opened the conversation with a remark about the cat sleeping on the papers. 'Oh yes, said the man, I've got two cats. That's Rhubarb, I think Custard's out in the garden.'

Again, years ago I distinctly remember watching the annual Crufts show on TV. There was a massive St Bernard dog who'd won a championship cup for Best in Class or something. He had the most wonderful name: Burtonswood Bossy-Boots. I've never forgotten it.

Anecdotes

I had an uncle and aunt who lived in Christchurch (near Bournemouth) whom we used to visit occasionally. He was very interesting to talk to; he was elderly then and sadly passed away many years ago. On one visit we'd got chatting about jobs he'd had in his youth. At one time he'd had a job on a car production-line. "When you took the car off the end of the line," he said, "you'd drive it round to the pumps and fill it up with petrol. But you had to leave the engine running, otherwise it would seize up and you couldn't start it again." I said "What make of car was that then?". "Oh" he said, "it was a Model T Ford".

He was also quite a character. Christchurch had just had a

new by-pass built and he used to complain about the traffic still going up the old main street. One day we were walking up that street on the way to his allotment and before I knew it he was yelling at all the cars (in his broad Hampshire accent) "Git out on the by-pass, darn yer."

Another story concerned the skipper of a fishing-boat moored in the harbour. Apparently he'd got drunk one night and fallen in the water. "Someone pulled 'n out" said my uncle. "Just as well, 'cos 'e couldn't swim."

Yet another story concerned a relative of his who had opened the first-ever cinema in Christchurch. He was also the projectionist and had got fed up with the constant flickering of all the films he was projecting. So he played around with the projector and "took the flicker out of 'un". Quite an unsung hero I'd say.

Out of the mouths of babes...

This was told to me as a true story, which I can well believe. A double-deck bus had got wedged fast under a low bridge. The police and fire brigade had struggled to free it for about two hours with no success. A small boy on his way home from school came up the road and stopped to take in the scene. Then he tapped one of the salvage crew on the shoulder; "Hey mister," he said, "Why don't you let the tyres down?" They did, and drove the bus out with no further trouble.

Philosophy of life

Life has its ups and downs. Some days you'll feel like the pigeon, other days you'll feel like the statue. If you can learn to deal with both those situations, it'll help you deal with life.

Keeping fit

Unfortunately I suffer from back trouble – I can't get it off the bed first thing in the morning. But I do exercise: Out of bed, up, down, up, down - I do this ten times - then the other eyelid. And I watch Emmerdale three times a week – if it wasn't for that I wouldn't get any fresh air at all.

Security

My quirky sense of humour means I love those security signs you see around saying 'This building is alarmed' or 'This car is alarmed'. My reaction to that is: 'Well, don't look at me, I didn't upset it.'

Selling

Another good one is those adverts in papers and magazines that say 'Send no money NOW!' I've never quite been able to work out how you do that.

And finally:
The rain it raineth on the Just
He who whispers down a well
And on the Unjust fella
About the goods he has to sell

But more upon the Just because
Will never make as many dollars
The Unjust steals the Justs umbrella.
As he who climbs a tree and hollers

CHAPTER 19
PRESENTABLE POEMS

I have called these Presentable Poems as that is a more preferable (and less boring!) title than just Comedy Poems. Although my poems may start out as 'ordinary', humour always seems to creep into them somehow, even to the extent that it sneaks in while I am not looking, so I need a better description.

The Bus Ride

Though in other ways I thrive
Unfortunately I cant drive
So, with some degree of fuss
I go out and catch a bus

I pass trees, houses, fields and grass
All courtesy of my Bus Pass

Then with no malice a-forethought
I espy a petrol forecourt
On it there's a glaring sign
'Unleaded £1.49'

That's each litre! When I try
To turn it into gallons, my
Store of knowledge just runs out
Its roughly - quite a small amount

OK, it's useless - you can laugh,
It's something like four and a half.
My brain, when faced with such a test
Falters, slows and comes to rest

Leaving me without an answer
I need some sort of brain-enhancer!
'Don't we all' I hear you cry
A hopeless statistician, I

To run a car, there's no relaxing
Insurance, service, road fund taxing
And as well as all of these
There are of course the breakdown fees

AA, Green Flag, RAC,
It all would be the death of me
Roadworks, queues, you end up waiting
I find that most excruciating

So, though I travel near and far
I'm glad that I don't need a car!

No More Metrication Please!

Maybe I'm just sentimental
But I've not gone continental

Thinking on it for a while
I never was a Europhile

At its edge, my brain just teeters
Over grammes, and millimetres

To me it makes so much more sense
To think in yards and pints and pence

Though 'metric feet' in timber's fine
Mine are still a shoe-size nine.

Though two metres it may be
I think of it as six feet three

Or something like that, I don't know
My bad maths now starts to show

At school I never found it hard
Three feet always was a yard.

I know where it's all coming from
But I am still confused dot com,

Oh, This Weather!

Rain, rain go away
Don't come again another day
If you looked hard I'm sure you'd find
A way to rain that we won't mind

Just when we think the dark sky's ended
We find the rain goes on extended

My garden's absolutely sodden
Everywhere that I have trodden

And the rest of it as well
Come, be honest, truth to tell
If you would just start thinking into it
You could stop me sinking into it
Our weather can be really joyous
Until you do things which annoy us

Like making rain run down our necks
It really is enough to vex
Even the most patient folk
We are always getting soaked
Usually without good reason
Even when it's out of season

You should be quite ashamed of that
Your rain's enough to drown a cat!
But as always I just do it
Get my mac on and walk through it
Other ways just might be better
And they'd stop us getting wetter
But you just bring torrential rain
Down upon our heads again

All the time my grass is growing
One thing's certain it needs mowing
And there's only me to do it
So with a will I jump right to it

I say that now but anyway
You can't believe all that I say
Its more like.. 'No, not that again
Maybe it will start to rain'

But really that puts off the task
An hour of sun is all I ask
So I can run the mower around
My unkempt scruffy piece of ground

Then the effort is worthwhile
I can permit myself a smile
The transformation is serene
Pathetic patch to bowling green!

Elastic Plastic

A thought, would it not be fantastic
If our money was elastic!
Then t'would stretch as far as needed
And our bills could go unheeded!

Thus they would be promptly paid
And not financially delayed
Causing us so much less stress
Our money then not in a mess

Then it would not be so drastic
Dealing with our daily plastic
Spending's easy but alack

Just you try and put it back!

Though I strive with might and main
My money still goes down the drain.
And thus it is that I remain
Bordering on the insane.

I wonder, will we ever be
Completely money-hassle-free?

(P.S. – Thought for today: Why is there always so much month left at the end of the money?)

The Helping Hand

With all your troubles, worries too
Anything that bothers you
Perhaps there's something I can do
To help you

You should not go through life alone
Or face your troubles on your own
You only have to lift the phone
Then I can help you

The stream of tears upon your face
I hope will cease at my embrace
And then smiles may take their place
Because I've helped you
When bad luck just will not abate

Whatever is decreed by fate
I will never hesitate
To help you

When things do not quite go to plan
I'd travel from a far-off land
Any time you need a hand
I'll come and help you

A helping hand is what I'll lend
I am not just a fleeting friend
I will be there until the end
To help you

If other people pass you by
Or just refuse to catch your eye
You know you always can rely
On me to help you

This is what true friends are for
I will knock upon your door
If I can possibly do more
To help you

You've been through bad times I guess
Your very soul I'll look to bless
If you're in an unholy mess
I can help you

You may think you've been forsaken
All your optimism taken
And your confidence is shaken
I can still help you

A rosy picture has been painted
But your view of life's been tainted
I can call upon some sainted
People who will help you

If you're dejected, wanting more
Adrift in life, can't reach the shore
Isn't that what friends are for?
I'm here to help you

To be here is what I intend
A sympathetic ear I'll lend
Perhaps your broken heart I'll mend
I'm honoured that you call me friend
That is why I'll always help you.

CHAPTER 20
THE LION'S SHARE

I am reliably informed (!) that the following conversation took place recently between one of the lions in Trafalgar Square and the adjacent one which was nearest to him. (You don't believe me? Shame on you - some people have no imagination!). In order to avoid boring names like Lion 1 and Lion 2 I shall call them Leo and Lionel.

Leo: Boring here isn't it?

Lionel: What d'you mean?

Leo: Well, same old routine, the tourists come round here, take pictures of us when we're not doing anything worth photographing, them they take pictures of themselves leaning on us or pretending to stick their fingers up our noses, then they go on to the next London landmark, then they go home.

Lionel: Well that picture you took of one the other day didn't go down so well did it?

Leo: Well what was I supposed to do when those twenty-five flies landed on my backside all at once? I had to get them off somehow.

Lionel: Well you didn't have to do THAT did you?

Leo: Can I help it if that tourist was standing so close to me?

Lionel: That wasn't the point – you swished your tail so hard you sent him flying head-first into the fountain.

Leo: Well I reckoned he needed a bath and it gave us a good laugh anyway.

Lionel: His mates weren't laughing...

Leo: Why not?

Lionel: Well three of them fell in the fountain while they were trying to get him out.

Leo: Anyway, I'm starving, I'm so hungry I could eat a whole sightseer right NOW! Look, there's a big fat juicy one just coming out of McDonald's...

Lionel: Oh will you stop it – you know we're not allowed to do that any more - that bloke from the Metropolitan Council was back again last week complaining.

Leo: Cant I even chew one up a bit?

Lionel: No!

Leo: Well can I just maul one about a bit then? I promise I wont hurt him very much. If he yells I'll just pick him up gently by the scruff of the neck and take him over to Charing Cross Hospital and dump him outside A &E, they'll take him in and fix him up and send him home and no-one will be any the wiser.

Lionel: No, you cant even do that.

Leo: Oh good grief, they don't let us have any FUN these days do they? If we can't attack the big tourists, how about one of the little ones, they wouldn't miss just one small one would they?

Lionel: Yes they would, you know the big ones always look after the small ones. They check how many small ones they've got when they leave home, then when they leave here they check the numbers again to make sure none of them have got lost or gone swimming in the fountain.

Leo: Oh yes, I'd forgotten that – that's dead sneaky that is - we don't stand a chance do we? We're not even allowed between-meal snacks now!

Lionel: Look I tell you what, just to keep you quiet, we'll play a game. You stay here and I'll nip over to Tesco's in the Strand, get a massive bottle of washing-up liquid and we'll pour it in the fountain.

Leo: Bubble-bath's better…

Lionel: Look, just stop it will you - you'll get us sent back to the jungle. Have you forgotten it's a tropical rain forest – you don't want to go back to that do you - getting drenched to the skin every couple of months?

Leo: Huh, the weather's nearly as bad as that here – we've had so much rain, that fountain's overflowed ten times this year already.

Lionel: Yes and look what happened the last time – we had to rescue that coach-load of tourists before they drowned!.

Leo: Well, we did it didn't we? I must say they weren't very grateful.

Lionel: Hardly surprising is it? You went dashing over to Buck House with them - Charles was not best pleased to see you lot turning up unexpectedly in his back garden.

Leo: What I don't understand why they all made such a fuss.

Lionel: What did you expect? They were all fine until you tried to peg them out on his washing-line to dry off. What made it worse was that he was in the middle of watching Coronation Street when you barged in.

Leo: I was only trying to help – I found out he was watching it on Catch-up anyway - he'd missed three episodes because of his own Coronation!

Lionel: Anyway, we'll have to watch what we do from now on or else you know what will happen – we'll get the ultimate punishment!

Leo: What's that then?

Lionel: You know what that is just as well as I do – they'll throw us both in the Tower!

CHAPTER 21
IT'S ALL ABOUT BUSES

I have now come to the inevitable conclusion that if you organise yourself, buses will work for you. If you don't. they'll work against you. The buses I rely on to get into 'town' only run once an hour (and not on Sundays). So I go out at the right time to catch one - that's the easy bit. Coming back, I invariably finish my shopping half an hour before my next bus back. So, I go into the Asda store (which is very close to the bus stop), nip into the toilet if I need to, then wander round the store (there's always something I've run out of - or about to) and make my way back to the bus stop at just the right time. However, it's essential to build in some contingency time in case there's a queue at the checkout! Even if there's no queue, the self-scan checkout may well tell you to 'Place the item in the bagging area' a second time because it failed to read it properly the first time you did it!!

Isn't it funny how when you're running late catching your bus you hurry to the bus stop hoping it hasn't gone (i.e. it's running late). But after you've waited quite a while you wish it would hurry up and come because you think you may have missed it. If it is running late, you're annoyed at being held up and getting to your destination late. It isn't until you get off it that you actually stop stressing about it.

We have 'quiet buses' where I live. At least that's what it says on the bus-times display at the bus stop shelters: 'Bus quiet'. The first time I saw it I thought it meant either that the bus was electrically-powered or that you couldn't use your mobile phone while you were on it. But no, it just meant that there weren't many people on it − mundane but actually more informative. However, I started wondering what they put on there when the bus was full-up − 'Bus loud' − no, I think not. Probably 'Bus full'. Let's face it, there wouldn't be room on the display-board for 'Standing room only' or 'Bus chock-a-block' or even 'Suggest you wait for the next one' now would there?

Funny How...

Isn't it funny how....

When you're rushing to catch a bus (and you're running late) you hope it hasn't turned up yet (if it has, maybe you've missed it). But when you get to the stop and it hasn't gone, then after a couple of minutes hanging around, you wish it would hurry up and come! It isn't until it finally arrives that you stop stressing about it.

A Bus Anecdote

I regularly go out with a lady friend of mine to a local shopping centre. I get on the No 8 bus and she gets on it where she lives which is about 6 stops farther on. We always catch the bus which leaves me at 1.30 and gets to her about 1.35. Last week

I got on it as normal but I noticed that the timetable that day was in a mess. Sure enough, a second No 8 appeared as if from nowhere right behind the one I was on.

This should not have been a problem. Unfortunately the two buses started to play a game commonly known as 'Bus Leapfrog', though I have a much less complimentary name for it. By the time my bus (lets call it bus No 1) had reached her stop it had become bus No 2, having been overtaken by the other one. However, she received Bus No 2 at her stop first (on its own), and naturally expected me to be on it. After checking it and finding me not there she was unexpectedly confronted by another no 8 (mine, though she didn't know it) which, having been thoroughly upset at being leap-frogged in the first place, had decided to retaliate.. Thus, she had no chance of checking the second No 8 (aka bus no 1 - the one I was on) which sailed past her in the process of leapfrogging Bus No 2 . I was not sure which (if either) of the buses she was on and the same applied in her case. The journey takes 45 minutes, so I'd better not elaborate on the remainder of it as I'm sure you can guess more or less what happened. To cut a long story short, we eventually did meet up at our usual café, and made a pact that in future, if we didn't manage to meet on the bus (for whatever reason) we would meet at the café and leave the buses to play games whenever they felt like it.

CHAPTER 22
PERVERSE POEMS

A Poem about Poetry

I do like writing poetry
Some days it just flows out of me
At other times its very taxing
Stops me totally relaxing

Though on occasions it wont scan
I'll make it fit whene'er I can
While making all of this stuff up, let's
Not forget the rhyming couplets
On which it all depends, you see
It still won't get the best of me

Writing poetry is fun
Though sometimes it may over-run
The page, the verse or just the line
Mostly it will work out fine.
(Just like that cliché, 'fine and dandy'
 Things like that come in quite handy!)

Though to some this may sound trite
I believe I get it right
You're reading it now aren't you? Well
I believe that time will tell

Though fame and fortune's all the rage
I would not like to be on stage
I'd stand there shaking, couldn't budge
My audience would be the judge

They'd say 'Look, we have had enough
Of your atrocious stand-up stuff '
There'd be a 'boo' or muttered cough
Meaning 'OK, now get off
The stage' but that won't worry me,
At least I'll get home for my tea

And biscuits (Though good for a rhyme
That joke wont work a second time!)

I might even dance or sing
Thinking I'm the greatest thing
Since sliced bread - that is much too vain
I'd not be welcome back again

I will always add a joke
While that might displease some folk
I may try to put a pun in it
Otherwise there is no fun in it

It's true that I am always wary
Sometimes it does get really scary
But I never get upset
By doggerel or epithet
Yet it's not easy, I must say

I do not like hyperbole
Since I found out that on the whole
It's mispronounced as 'hyper-bole'

If that's true even half the time
Just how then can I make it rhyme?

I'm So Much Cleaner Now

I had a shower yesterday
So now my social life's OK
It's true I don't smell any more
At least, not like I did before
I had it

Nice smells now leave a better scene
In all the places I've just been
And gone from

It's a fact, I knew I'd sinned
With people crossing roads up-wind
Of me
In order to avoid the pong
I realised it had lasted long
Enough

The Council too were on my back
Complaining of my woeful lack
Of hygiene
They wrote 'Your nuisance value is too great
We've had umpteen complaints of late
About you'

But now I've got the ladies raving
With my trendy after-shaving
Previously I'd scared them stiff
Now all they need is just one whiff
Of me
Now any female conversation
In any cosy quiet location
Starts 'Hey Handsome, you are cute
With that enticing smell of Brut

Or if it's not, I'm at a loss
Is it that one by Hugo Boss?
Or on reflection, no, methinks
It could be Africa by Lynx

Or maybe its Imperial Leather
Either way, it's been a pleasure
Meeting you.'

Relationships develop now
That I am realising how
My body odour has diminished
No longer do my amours finish
After just one whiff

In fact they go on getting stronger
And they last a whole lot longer
Than they did

Who knows, one day, come stormy weather
We might even shower together.
Though some might say 'You didn't oughter.'
The main thing is, we're saving water!

All I Want is You

While pottering in my garden shed,
Or when I'm in the loo.
You are always in my head
'Cos all I want is you

I hated going shopping
You spent all my cash, it's true
I've got much more of it now
But all I want is you

You hated all the football
That I watched on Channel 2
I've lost track of every match
Yet all I want is you

I couldn't stand your mother
And I'm sure she loathed me too
She used to come round every day
I only wanted you

We used to argue constantly
The neighbours heard us too.
Who am I going to yell at
Now I don't have you?

Your constant nagging deafened me
Your stomach noises too
But now its just a deathly hush
Still all I want is you
Your liaison with the coalman
Now that wasn't something new,
Extra sacks weren't all he left
He left you pregnant too

I'd suspected it for ages
But I didn't need to say
It was the filthy hand-prints on the towels
That gave it all away

This all built up within my mind
And things were getting hectic
It was only when he'd been six times
I realised we're all-electric

Your dalliance with the postman
I overlooked that too
He would debate the postage rates
So he could speak to you

I didn't like the way he smiled
And he was always humming
He looked like Robert Redford
So I should have seen it coming

I'm Stuck in the Sixties

I love to spend time playing my
Super sixties loud hi-fi

Though it's all ancient history now
It all comes back to me somehow
I'm happier than I've ever been
I'm loving it, I dig the scene

I can't sit and watch a movie
I have to get all hep and groovy
The music could be sweet and low
But never on my stereo!

I think that's why hi-fi was made
To put out huge great blasts of Slade.
But now I have a reputation
I cause many a sensation

What's that loud persistent beat?
I cause problems in our street
All the neighbours crowding round
My house all yelling 'Turn it down!'

What's the cause? Could it be my
Ghetto-blasting, loud hi-fi?
Or the music that I might
Play all day long and half the night?

With my windows open wide
I should really run and hide!

The neighbours just don't like me playing
Solid beat, they're always saying
'I wish he'd take a rest - oh no,
He's putting on more Status Quo!'

Or, 'Oh good grief, whatever next ?
He knows that we can't stand T-Rex!'
Just because they've never been
Part of the sixties 'swinging scene'

Queen's a band that far excels
Most others, but their decibels
Float for miles right down the road
Causing ear-drums to explode

And next, to get them all annoyed
Something inventive by Pink Floyd
Or else I'll help them 'get it on'
With something by Roy Orbison

There is one group I think they'll know
And like, and that is ELO
But I am sure that they will be
Entranced when they hear 10cc

Passers-by are heard to say
'I heard your noise ten streets away'
Maybe I'll turn it down and grab a
Nice cool soothing time with Abba

Before I get an ultimatum
I must try and educate 'em
Bring them round with all this plastic
Soon they'll think its just fantastic!

Now then I just wonder where
I put that CD of Cher
Or maybe I will just put on
Something soothing – Elton John?

So as not to cause a riot
I will look for something quiet.
Loud cacophony must cease
Before they call the Noise Police

They will come and clobber me
A small lad (only five feet three)
Though I might just try and run
I'd have two chances, slim and none

They'd call me a rebellious male
Then just throw me into jail.
Hoping I'd repent my sins
Life has losses, not all wins!

Contemplating what I'd got:
Head still pounding, eardrums shot
Though it's music that is 'hot'
Was it worth it? No. p'raps not!

Man's Inhumanity to Man

All the battles and the strife
The disregard for human life
And the drones which cause such harm
Without an adequate alarm
Every day more pain and trouble
Buildings now just piles of rubble

Explosions, people running scared
Caught unaware and unprepared.
Hospitals that should bring hope
Now still try but cannot cope
Many wounded, many tears
Many live in mortal fear
Lest they should be wrongly caught
In the next perverse onslaught

We seem to hear this more each day
And yet we cannot turn away
Just deny it if you can
Man's inhumanity to man.

Such antagonistic factions
Demand more sensible reactions

Is it really any wonder
Peace now has been torn asunder?

It's time to turn the tide, we should
Act now for the common good
To foster more humane relations
Nation should speak peace to nation
Improving on what went before
Deny henceforth the need for war

This was surely not our plan
For Man's humanity to man.
Instead of watching buildings burn
We should think and plan and learn

Can we not learn from past mistakes
And a harmonious future make?
Acting now far less erratic
Enacting plans more diplomatic
Could an all-pervading plan
Cement the brotherhood of man?

Would it so much wound our pride
If we were now to put aside
Actions which cause so much pain
Can we not live in peace again?

.We must consider now the need
To repent of past misdeeds
And moving forward take a pride

In having made a useful stride

While we persist in hard exchanges
Day by day the climate changes
Always making weather worse
Yet we continue so perverse.

All nations should contrive a plan
For man's HUMANITY to man

CHAPTER 23
RANDOM RABBITTING

Thought for today: Why should cats have it all their own way?

DOGAPULT
A small slingshot-type weapon which automatically retrieves its own missiles.

DOGALOGUE
A list of all known doggy sniffs and smells, each with a detailed description.

DOGASTROPHE
A critical situation which demands immediate attention, usually in the form of copious tummy-rubs.

DOGALYTIC CONVERTER
A small machine which converts your car horn and parking sensor so that they both emit barking sounds.

The cats fight back!

CATMATIC
A person who is rather annoying because they are purrfect! Worse, they always know correct way to do things., for example, how to catch mice.

CAT-TIRED
Feeling so tired that you could curl up and sleep in a very small basket.

CAT ROSE

A rose that has claws instead of thorns.

CAT-EARED

An item that is furry and scruffy having been used a lot, probably to catch mice. (Note, the remains of a ball of wool also fall into this category.

CAT COLLAR

A clerical collar (possibly worn by lady vicars?), usually pink and sparkly.

Anecdotes

I have a friend who is Irish. I don't hold that against him – in fact it's a bonus! He is typically Irish which means, firstly that he can talk for England (or rather, Ireland!) and secondly that he has a fantastic sense of humour.   He recently went into hospital to have a pacemaker fitted. He told me he was on the operating table for four hours; I said 'That must have been uncomfortable for you'. 'No. not really' he said, 'I missed most of it.' I said 'How was that then?' He replied: 'I was asleep!'

Once at a party I met an Irish chap who had a great sense of humour, in fact he was absolutely hilarious. We were talking about the weather and somehow the subject of pine-cones crept into the conversation. He said 'Did you know you can use those to tell what the weather is like?' I said no. 'Oh well' he said 'you put a pinecone in the gutter above your back door, and if it falls on your head when you go out, you know it's windy!'.

Later on, the subject of gourmet meals came up. He said 'Have you ever tried Poulet Maserati?' I said 'No, what is it?' He replied 'It's chicken that has been run over in the road'

I was chatting to a close neighbour and I asked what his favourite hobby was.

'Oh,' he said 'I keep racing pigeons.' I said 'Oh yes and do you win very often?'

He said ,No, hardly at all, they can fly a bit faster than I can.' It turned out they were homing pigeons. I said 'Where do you fly them to?' He said 'Barcelona.' I thought, that's a long way to go just to indulge your favourite hobby.

Thoughts to make you think

Tomorrow is the first day of the rest of your life.

A smile can say a hundred words - try using a smile and words together – the effect can be devastating.

The smallest kindness can reap the greatest rewards.

In life today, people are so quick to criticise and so slow to praise. We should all aim to redress that balance.

Of all the things I've lost – I miss my mind the most.

I love hard work – I can watch it all day.

I don't like chocolate – I love it.
We only have one life – always try to use it wisely.

Exploding Soup

I had Exploding Soup for lunch the other day. That wasn't what it was called on the tin, but I didn't cover it when I put it in the microwave. Halfway through cooking I heard a muffled thump from the microwave, so I stopped to check it out. There was more soup all over the inside of the microwave than was left in the dish

Me and my (bad) memory

I worry sometimes I could be losing my memory. Well, when you're retired and living on your own all the days seem the same somehow. I have woken up on Wednesday thinking it's Thursday and because of that I missed a coffee morning with one of my two social clubs. On another occasion, I had the right day but I was running an hour early without realising it, and as a result I phoned my cleaning lady thinking maybe she was ill and wasn't coming when in fact there was nothing wrong. I have an idea that I might get myself a name-badge – this won't be to tell people who I am, it'll be in case I forget my own name.

I recently lost my bus-pass, That was worse than it sounds, because, not being able to drive, I rely heavily on it to get around. I spent a couple of (fruitless) days looking for it, then applied for a new one which didn't come for a week! So, a total of 9 days virtually housebound without it, plus a £14 admin fee. I never did find it. I shan't do that again in a hurry!

I also left my wallet on a bus – luckily I got it back intact – all my credit cards survived, plus (miraculously!) £140 in cash. I have also left my car keys in peoples cars (twice!) and in spite of not being able to retrieve it before they drove off, all ended well in both cases, though I did get a right ribbing from my social club mates about that!

Funny How

Isn't it funny that before my cleaning lady comes I always rush around the house clearing up and tidying up? I'm thinking 'Can't have her seeing the house in this state' The only trouble is that when I have tidied up, if I want something afterwards I cant remember where I put it. And if I drop any cereal on the floor while eating my breakfast I clean it up myself right away!

I have taken a liking to honey-nut clusters for breakfast, but I have to take a sledgehammer to the bigger ones before I can eat them (note, I exaggerate for effect - it's called poetic, or in this case, prosaic licence). I did actually break some up with a hammer once, just so I could say that I'd done it. (Couldn't resist that with my warped sense of humour!)

Isn't it funny how you hardly ever read the leaflets that come with your medicines and tablets. But every once in a while, you think it's about time you read it properly because you have to remind yourself what it's doing to you and/or which bit of you it's supposed to be treating.

Note: if you have said 'Yes, I do that' to any of the above items, don't worry, you don't need a psychiatric test − it just means you're normal!

There's always one...

There's always one key that you find in your house that wont fit anything. You try it in about 6 places where it should fit but it doesn't. But you've got to keep it because you know darn well that if you don't, you will find out the hard way that it fits something very important!

There's always one big object in your house that you never use and/or don't really like. You would rather have its space than its company and you want to get rid of it. But it's too big to take to the charity shop, so you try and think of a use for it, and while you're doing that you leave it where it is.

There's always one person on a bus or train who thinks you need to hear his or her conversation from beginning to end, and they act as if they are happy for you to join in but you know that you thoroughly disagree with what they're saying, so it might annoy them or make them even louder.

There's always one tablet short when you're getting your medicines ready to take, but you have to work out which one it is by looking at all the others.

When you're telling one of your best jokes there's always one person in the room who, while all the others are falling about with laughter, looks blankly at you and says 'Sorry, I dont get it or 'what do you mean?'

Dictionary
The dictionary that I used while I was writing this book describes itself as follows:

"The Oxford Concise Dictionary: Over 8,000 references. 113,000 definitions"

On measuring it, I noticed it is 2.5 inches thick! This inevitably strikes a chord in the 'supreme irony' department of my brain. If this is the concise version, I hate to think how big it was before they started working on it to reduce it!

CHAPTER 24
SILLY VERSE FOR ADULTS
(Why should the kids have all the fun?)

Wippity woppity oh what a pain
Take care lest your brolly should fall down a drain
Wippity woppity cuddly pup
Cos if it goes down you can't get it back up
Wippity woppity devil to pay
You can struggle all night, you can struggle all day
Wippity woppity hot treacle pud
But once it's gone down then you've lost it for good.

Higgledy piggledy sixpence a throw
A centurion tank just ran over my toe
Higgledy piggledy syrup of figs
That has really put paid to me dancing fast jigs
Higgledy piggledy can't hear the bell
Waltzes and cha-chas and tangos as well
Higgledy piggledy pleasure-enhancing
But then I always was rubbish at dancing

Huffity puffity back of the net
I really do hate going out when it's wet
Huffity puffity slept like a log
But it doesn't matter 'cos so does the dog.
Huffity puffity over the moon
Or when it's blowing a howling typhoon
Huffity puffity wow that is big
If there's one thing I hate it is losing my wig.

Hummable drummable pasta tray bake
I did some fishing in our local lake
Hummable drummable oodles of lolly
For starters I fished out an old Asda trolley
Hummable drummable living in sin
I was doing alright 'til I slipped and fell in
Hummable dummable bad hacking cough
But I soon got out and I dried myself off

Wimbling wombling quick as you like
And then I fished out a rusty old bike
Wimbling wombling that cat's a stray
I suddenly realised I'd been there all day
Wimbling wombling lo and behold
And I'd only caught two tin cans and a cold
Wimbling wombling don't spill that cup
Now I've decided to give it all up

Willaby wallaby this shelf needs dusting
The weather round here has been really disgusting
Willaby wallaby rocking-horse brain
For about three weeks now we've had nothing but rain
Willaby wallaby yes it's your shout
Well I wouldn't mind but you just cant get out

Knicketty knacketty going insane
They're always saying its quicker by train
Knicketty knacketty go take a hike
But check it out first 'cos they're always on strike
Knicketty knacketty vicars and tarts

Anyone fancy a quick game of darts?
Knicketty knacketty hate growing old
I'm simply freezing, this weather's so cold

Shillying shallying baked beans on toast,
If there's one thing I like it's a nice Sunday roast
Shillying shallying round and about
Complete with some stuffing and small Brussels sprouts
Shillying shallying don't join the Navy
And to top it all off there has got to be gravy
Shillying shallying you bet your life
Otherwise peas will just roll off your knife

Argying bargying got to be frugal
I know its the truth cos I checked it on Google.
Argying bargying turned down the heat
But my bungalow now is as cold as the street
Argying bargying don't want to freeze
So bought a new jumper that covers my knees
Argying bargying cold wind is blowing
Don't know where it's from but I know where it's going
Argying bargying rude girls and vicars
Could be my fault, I forgot to wear knickers

Wippity woppity just one more thing
I wanted to say and that's God Save the King!

CHAPTER 25
BACKWORD
(Opposite of Foreword)

I may write further poems yet
But for now these are the best you'll get
Or prose, who knows what life will bring?
It could be almost anything

I hope that you enjoyed my stuff
And that it was good enough
To make you laugh, or make you smile
And cheer you up for just a while

I leave you now, but know that this is
With my very best good wishes
I wish you happiness and rest
And hope your life will be the best.

Lastly:
Be happy
Be strong
Be positive
Keep well
Keep safe
Keep loving

AND ABOVE ALL: **KEEP LAUGHING!**